I Am His Daughter

Valerie A. Burrell

Nina Y. Williams

Unless otherwise indicated, all scriptural quotations are from the King James Version or the Message version of the Bible.

Published by
Valerie A. Burrell
empowermentplc@gmail.com

empowermentplc@gmail.com

Cover design: Savannah Carabin, Carabin Designs
Art: Lu Miranda, KinArt Wraps

Second Edition

Printed in the United States of America

DEDICATION

This book is dedicated to the memory of our parents, William and Barbara. To our children, who are our heartbeats and our legacy. May you always know that regardless of what comes to life- you matter!

To those of you who have been challenged in your identity because of an absent parent, we hope that this book will give your voice back, as it's been silent for too long. We pray that you will experience validation for every thought and emotion, realizing that none of what you experienced was your fault.

We desire that as this book empowers you, you will take the responsibility to empower others.

Live an Empowered Life!

FOREWORD

As the husband of Valerie Burrell and brother-in-law of Nina Williams, I have seen the residuum in their lives, a legacy of their parents. Their ability to fulfill their purpose with a Kingdom mindset has allowed them to overcome what others view as obstacles. Their growth and obedience to the Word of God have given them great insight to help others prevail. This book will serve as a conduit for others to realize their purpose.

Benny M. Burrell, Author
Justified Silence

FROM THE AUTHORS

You never know how the passing of a loved one is truly going to affect you until it happens. For us, the passing of our father created moments of tension, confusion, heart woes, and even anger. You see, our father hadn't been a critical player in our life, but in his final days, emotions were tested, but I'm grateful that we kept sin at bay.

We are grateful for our family, friends, and all the love shown to us and the prayers prayed during this moment in life. Thank you, family, for your constant support and encouragement in the process. We've experienced many joys and woes on this journey, and you'll have given us strength every step of the way.

In the pages of this book, we share our accounts with hopes to encourage someone else who may have an estranged relationship with their father. If you're in that position, please release your thoughts and emotions to start your healing process. What God has done for us is a marvelous thing, and He can do the same thing for you as well.

CONTENTS

Dedication
Foreword
From the Authors

Our Father
William Taliaferro

!

1 YOU BASTARD

"No bastard is to enter the congregation of GOD, even to the tenth generation, nor any of his children."
Deuteronomy 23:2 (MSG)

You bastard! Have you ever been angry at a person and yelled at them, "You bastard!", Without really knowing how your words impact their opinion of self? As an adult, these words might be easily brushed off, but as a child, those words could begin to set you apart and often dictate the path of one's future. Proverbs 18:21 (NKJV) reads, *"Death and life are in the power of the tongue, and those who love it will eat its fruit."* Think about it; you've been placing a sentence on someone's life out of ignorance, malice, or even your sorrow.

How are you expected to function in a society when you're not confident who your father is and, in turn, not know who you are either? These are the questions we will begin to address as we examine the importance of a relationship with our earthly father.

For a period in my childhood – I didn't know who my father was. I was born of a woman who wasn't married to my biological father. So I was born on and labeled by this world, a bastard! The truth is- he was married to someone else, maybe not at the time of conception but to another woman who was also carrying his child. Juicy stuff, right? Not really; this was a typical occurrence, taking place all too often and hidden under a bush, sending the children to live with relatives up North or some other creative way of not disclosing the "truth" of the matter.

A bastard by Merriam Webster's definition is "a person born of parents not married to each other." That's something to carry around as a child, not having a complete understanding of what took place regarding my conception but now having to face society, scared. The word "bastard" alone sounds negative, but understanding the real meaning could initiate either joy or hurt. The synonyms: illegitimate child, love child; could prove to be confusing as well. Illegitimate signifies being unlawful, while love child would mean just that; created out of the desire to love and be loved by another – and if this was my start, then it wasn't as bad as the world would have me to believe.

I was called a bastard by those I knew and encountered as a child. They said this about me with no remorse and, as I recall, with a degree of disdain – as if I had something to do with my existence. Whew!!! I have to pause for a moment; reliving those moments causes a stir in me now that I couldn't have explained as a child.

A bastard! That term carried so many thoughts of not being wanted or even loved, but how the story changed. I remember being asked as a child, "Who is your daddy?" and I couldn't answer. All I remember ever stating was that my mother was Barbara. People will often ask who your parents are as a way to find out your lineage or possible relation to them, but some will question with the intent to disqualify you or make you feel unworthy.

As a child, you cannot discern the intent

behind the question, yet you are left to deal with its repercussions. Did it matter to people if they knew who my dad was? Did everybody know I was a bastard and were mocking me? Is that why I was treated differently? Frankly, my ability to recant these moments is monumental in our path of acceptance. We were born into a relationship of two individuals who had "moments of expressed love" yet are now suffering because of their inability to be what they desired.

As a student of the word of God, I became interested in the spiritual aspects of being a bastard. Deuteronomy 23:2 reads, "*No one of illegitimate birth shall enter the assembly of the LORD; none of his descendants, even to the tenth generation, shall enter the assembly of the LORD.*" The curse of the bastard is severe and applies even if parents wed before the child was born. This curse would have been applied to us, our parents, and could've gone down ten generations had it not been for Jesus' shed blood on Calvary. Because of our relationship with our heavenly Father – the curse was released! I'm confident that it carried over into our daily existence on the earth more than we realized.

Our conception and birth into this world were set to deliver demise and shame for us as children, but our awareness later in life awakened us into a truth of our identity. In yielding our will to our heavenly Father, we realized that who we were identified as in our childhood was not our truth. Jeremiah 1:5 shares, *"Before I formed you in the womb I knew you, before you were born I set you apart; I appointed you as a prophet to the nations."* (NIV) God called us to be His empowered vessels and has delivered us from the "bastard curse" to live on purpose. Let me suggest this to you; if you've called someone a "bastard" with no thought of the harm it caused or you are seeking the truth about who your earthly father is and harbor ill will towards your mother for not disclosing your reality, take a moment to pray this prayer:

Father, I come before you now asking for forgiveness. I realize now that what I spoke may have harmed a child or an adult, as I gave no thought to what I was speaking. I see now the power of my words and can't take them back. Father, I ask you also to come into my heart, allow me to forgive what I felt to be an injustice towards me. Father, you can wipe that slate clean, and I'm coming before you with that petition. Cleanse my heart and mind, create a clean heart, renew the right spirit in me, and send healing to the one I may have offended and healing to me. I ask this in Jesus' name. Amen

Were You labeled as a "bastard" or used that term to refer to someone else? Do you feel differently about it now? If so, how?

_____

_____

_____

_____

_____

_____

_____

_____

_____

_____

_____

_____

2 I KNOW, BUT I'M NOT KNOWN

For now, we see in a mirror dimly, but then face to face;
now I know in part, but then I will know fully
just as I also have been fully known.
1 Corinthians 13:12

I arrived at the funeral home for my grandfather's service on the arm of my dad, and the question is posed to him by his aunts and uncles, "Is that your new girlfriend?" and his response is, "No, this is my daughter." Can you imagine the look on our faces! His face, the picture of sheer embarrassment, and there I stood in disbelief, embarrassed and confused – all at the same time. It wasn't just the look on my face, but their faces as well! Was it because of his past and the vast number of women he'd had? It's as if they were speaking with their mouths closed; how could she exist and we not know? It's not like I was an infant or even a little kid, heck – I was an adult. Did they not see the resemblance of a smile or our eyes…why would his girlfriend be the first question they'd ask seeing us together?

Baffled as I was at the moment, I had to gather myself and embrace these beautiful people who were my great aunts and uncles for the first time. At that moment, I was reminded of the time my grandfather was in the hospital before he passed away, and I would drive my dad and some of my granddad's friends to visit during his last days. I would always be questioned, "Are you related to him?" At times, I wanted to respond with a harsh word, but what would it matter. Most of the world didn't know who I was and how I was connected – and I had the nerve to be acting shocked because my great aunts and uncles didn't know who I was.

Why? I kept asking myself, why? I was born just a few months after dad's first child. Was I supposed to be a secret? Get ready world, if you don't know who I am, brace yourself because there is another one that looks just like me that came a few years later – I thought to myself. The remainder of that day, as I recall, was a bit tense. My dad is looking at me as if he wanted to apologize for what had been said, yet there were no words that could erase that moment. Had this been a moment of awakening for my father? Was he now regretting his decision not to be in our lives? That day, I didn't get any answers, no show of remorse, but I got brief interactions with individuals who were my cousins from up north that I'd never met before.

The saying, "What's done in the dark will certainly come to light," was unfolding right before our eyes. Don't fool yourself, people; if there is a skeleton in your closet, do yourself a favor and deal with it now proactively instead of just waiting it out because they always have a way of revealing themselves. We've all done things in the past that we hope that no one will ever reveal, but trust that it will be known.

At this moment, whether the world was ready or not, "truth" was coming to light, not just for me but also for my dad. John 8:32

reads, "*Then you will know the truth, and the truth will set you free.*" Those uncomfortable moments at my grandfather's funeral were probably the genesis of my acceptance, and at that time, I couldn't see it.

What I faced was not out of the ordinary, based on societal norms. I'm sure that for anyone who has grown up with their mother, grandparents, or other family members and never got to spend time with their father or family, you can understand my emotions. Growing up, I remember spending a few days, which were few and far between, with my father and his "other family." I didn't spend time on the holidays, not even my birthday. I believe that had my father not been reminded, he wouldn't have even remembered when my birthday was. As a child, I never had a Thanksgiving dinner or Christmas sleepover with him and his other children, I knew about them, yet I knew nothing about them. My brother shared with me as adults that he thought that I was his "girlfriend" who came over to visit now and then. Although it sounds cute, in reality, it's unfortunate.

Bear with me, these emotions tend to flare up, and I have to deal with them at the moment. What I dealt with, not being known, all started from a relationship between two schoolmates, a relationship that carried on for more years than any of us could imagine, and according to my father, by love. How then, if it was love, could a father deny or dismiss his children. Why was it not okay for people to know all of his children? As Nina and I continued to grow and have a greater understanding of our existence, it was clear that we were outsiders, and it was so much deeper than what we were experiencing. There were emotions attached to our existence. Our mother was feeling some way. Our father was feeling some way. His ex-wife was feeling some way, and I find out in my adult life that some of the other children were and are still feeling some way. So we have to be punished and shunned because we didn't want to offend someone else? Did you give thought to that before you made us? Whew!

Blended families are typical in today's society. Based on the relationship, you hear parents refer to the children as, these are your children, my children, and our children, but when it came to how we were recognized by my dad and his circle of influence, we were known as "them, or Barbara's kids." That recognition or lack thereof accompanied a sense of being only but not belonging. As I've learned more about my father's family, I question whether this behavior could have been attached to some generational stuff in our family? Were there more stories of uncertainty that lingered, and no one was mentioning them either?

As many years passed, our father began to be open about his thoughts towards us. I could feel his desire to share with the world that we were "his" children. No more hiding behind what was done so many years ago! I recall that in my early 40's, he approaches me about getting my birth certificate updated, listing him as my father. Why? After all these years - now you want to put your name on a document to acknowledge paternity! Who cared at the point? I had to come to terms with the fact that he did!

I'm not sure whether this was due to health challenges he was beginning to face and his time winding down or whether he felt compelled now to share in our life experiences in hopes of making up for what we had lost. Regardless of his intent, this didn't happen. He desired to eliminate any obstacles that could surface when he transitioned as if he knew what we'd face.

REFLECTIONS or THOUGHTS
Do you have or know someone that struggles from not being acknowledged by their father?

_____

_____

_____

_____

_____

_____

_____

_____

_____

_____

_____

_____

3 GETTING TO KNOW YOU

"But now, thus says the LORD, your Creator, O Jacob, And He who formed you, O Israel, "Do not fear, for I have redeemed you; I have called you by name; you are Mine!"
Isaiah 43:1 (NASV)

What's your favorite color? Who was your best friend in high school? What type of car do you like to drive? What's your favorite food? These are all simple questions, but do we know the answers regarding our siblings or children? Some of us will be able to answer these questions right off the bat; others may have to think about it for a minute or two; my dad couldn't answer any of them. With someone you spend time with daily, these nuisances you pick up on without thought. You know your oldest likes the color green but has relationship phobias; your middle child loves sports but lacks direction about what his future holds; your baby boy loves sesame chicken Chinese food but has issues with saving money. Time and closeness allow you to know these things about your family. Now imagine as an adult being asked these questions by a parent? I was laughing internally, my little stuff – and you're curious. For all these years, you didn't know, and it didn't matter, why now?

Getting to know someone takes time and effort. It's the work that determines whether this newfound information will benefit you down the road, but it's the time that makes it meaningful. Our Family Reunion in 2015 was a massive part of my "Getting to Know You." Not only am I learning about my father, but his father, and his father before him; aunts, uncles, cousins…all the same, yet so new and unknown to me. How was I to know that I shared lineage with an ex-spouse? Family reunion, 2015 – what an experience! As a descendant of the late Elizabeth Robinson, my husband and I attended this grand affair with my father, and to put it mildly – it was a bit overwhelming. Why was I looking at people who, as I was growing up, harshly entreated me, and now I find out that we're related! What's even worse is that I find out that my first husband and I are of the same lineage. Secrets of my existence were unfolding and revealing some murky waters. I would've never known this truth, our great history and legacy – had I not pursued this opportunity to know more, and this time he agreed.

So many people don't care to know what their family lineage holds, and unfortunately, it's the good, bad, and indifference that holds us back. Not only is it essential for building a stronger family foundation, but it also plays a role in your health. What types of disease is my family suffering from? What are the generational curses that are attached to us? What areas of the world have we migrated from? These are things that can only be discovered if you put in the time and effort to get to know them, and they get to know you.

So the phone rings, and you look at the caller id, and it says "DAD." Do you pick it up with a smile on your face knowing that just last year, it may have read his name instead of a title, or do you just let it ring and say to yourself, "I'll call him back later...or what does he want"? It's a simple thing, but if it's something you've not had – it's a moment to cherish. You answer with a smile, excited to hear his voice with him only to say, "I hadn't heard your voice in a few days and wanted to check on you." It's those calls that you cherish, and we will remember, now that he's gone.

Building this relationship with our earthly father should have been an easy process, but we often found it more challenging than building our relationship with God.

That if you confess with your mouth Jesus as Lord, and believe in your heart that God raised Him from the dead, you will be saved; 10 for with the heart a person believes, resulting in righteousness, and with the mouth, he confesses, resulting in salvation
Romans 10:9

Isn't that something? By confessing with my mouth and believing in my heart, the transformation began. I began walking in the newness of life and understanding who I am in a relationship with my heavenly Father. The time and effort needed in this relationship are like any other. God requires us to spend time with Him in prayer, fasting, fellowship, and the study of His Word. He knows every hair on our head, yet He awaits our invitation to commune with us and begins the life-changing relationship that will benefit every area of our lives – even the relationship with my earthly father.

Being in ministry was an avenue used by God to open the opportunity of us really "knowing" our earthly father. Before ministry assignments, I didn't hang out much with my father except for the old cabarets at the Van Den Boogaard Center back in the day or a car show – here or there. When he heard that I was a minister, it piqued an interest in him. I'm not sure whether it presented an opportunity to boast because I was his or because he was seeking something from God, and I may have been the vessel to aid him in finding it. Regardless of the reason, my father readily received the word from the Lord when

I would minister and would come to the altar for prayer each time, seeking answers and healing.

James Rowe wrote one of my favorite hymns, "Love, Lifted Me," in 1912, and love has proven to be the key to the building of our family "unit." Love, the emotional choice of acceptance beyond criticism or judgment, is what opened our hearts to change us from what we'd been to make us into what God desired we be – FAMILY! Love was restoring to my biological father what he'd abandoned in not fully acknowledging us, and we were healing of hurt inflicted by his choices to please society instead of pleasing God. Not a day in my life did my father train me or instill anything in me to aid me in navigating life, but he taught me through his actions. As a mother of three beautiful women, I vowed at their birth to be more to them than I'd received, and I'm grateful to God for being able to pour into each of them.

REFLECTIONS or THOUGHTS

_____

_____

_____

_____

_____

_____

_____

_____

_____

_____

_____

_____

,

4 TRANSITIONING INTO A HEALTHY PLACE

Finally, brethren, whatever is true, whatever is honorable, whatever is right, whatever is pure, whatever is lovely, whatever is of good repute, if there is any excellence and if anything worthy of praise, dwell on these things
Philippians 4:8

What is a healthy relationship? Based on who you ask, you'll get different versions of their reality which often does not speak to the truth of what "healthy" is. A healthy relationship defined by a battered spouse may be, but he/she loves me, I just did something wrong," or I don't want to be alone, so I put up with whatever happens. A healthy relationship with self could include; dealing with eating disorders, drug and alcohol abuse, physical abuse, and sexual addiction, still claiming to be healthy. Finding wholeness of self is the key to being able to build healthy relationships with others. As parents, we carry the weight of instilling the "right" things in our children to expect that they will adhere to the teachings, obey us and live successful lives.

Do we condemn them for fulfilling or satisfying their flesh, knowing that we were doing the same thing not too long ago, or do we allow them to learn independently? For most, the relationship you have with your parents is your first. You depend on your parents to feed, nurture and teach you right from wrong. What happens when the individual doesn't know how to parent and present what's needed?

I've learned as a parent that your children learn and understand more than we give them credit for. Sending a child to their room does not protect them from arguments or fighting. They can see the visible bruises and the looks of complete shame or embarrassment. Is this the example of marriage you want to portray? Does mommy need to cry every night; does daddy need a cold beer in his hand? The images leave an everlasting impression, but many parents lose sight of the adverse effects of their behavior.

How many of you grew up, like me, not spending any time with your biological father? Do you harbor feelings of resentment, or were you lucky enough to have someone else step in and provide you with the guidance you needed? For many, a healthy relationship is simply one in which you are free to express your thoughts, concerns, feelings and still feel loved.

Let's take an inventory of our thoughts during this time of transitioning into a healthy place:

- Am I pretty enough?
- Do I need to lose some weight?
- Do I look like any of my siblings?
- Do they want a relationship with us?

Every aspect of life that I viewed led to more self-doubt and fear of not being good enough and not being accepted. Add those concerns with not being part of your biological father's life, and then all of a sudden – he's there – as if he's been a constant.

Emotionally, transitioning into a healthy place in this relationship with my father took a toll on me. I don't think it was selfish of me to consider my emotions during this process – I was hurting, but there were days when I wondered about my siblings. How are they coping with his desire to embark upon building this new relationship with us? Will resentment surface? Will his love for us diminish how they express their love for him? The unanswered questions and reality of present conditions could prove explosive if not handled appropriately. In these moments, our relationship with our Heavenly Father gives guidance in embracing relationships with others in your life.

Transitions require forgiveness, not only of self but for others. When a child realizes that their parent is not "perfect" and not the fixer of everything, a shift occurs. Not only are you faced with coming to the reality of who you are, but of who your parents are not.

Hearing the three simple words, I Love

You, was taking on a new meaning. Knowing that someone loves you unconditionally can heal a broken heart. A relationship that was once unknown is now one that brings joy and provides radiance in your life, still includes joys and sorrow. In our case, the revelation didn't occur until a loved one passes on. So again, you are left to deal with the struggles of others as you come into your own true identity.

The transition happened; our father passed away. A few days prior, our siblings and I stood by his bed to share what the doctors were stating and listened as he shared his heart with each of us. His departure was preparing for each of us a place of healing.

REFLECTIONS or THOUGHTS

_____

_____

_____

_____

_____

_____

_____

_____

_____

_____

_____

_____

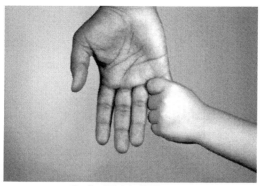

5 A FATHER

As a father has compassion on his children, so the LORD has compassion on those who fear him;
Psalm 103:13

Who is your father? Suppose you ask that question of me today. In that case, my response will come forth with ease and confidence, for I not only know who my earthly father was but am very aware of who my heavenly Father is and the benefits attached to that relationship. John 1:12 reads, "But to all who did receive him, who believed in his name, he gave the right to become children of God." Because of my adoption by God, it has given me rights to an inheritance that I won't have to fight for, seeks a lawyer for, or even depend on a written will for the release. My adoption by God is a Kingdom gift that every person willing to acknowledge and receive Him is entitled to.

What is a father? By definition, it is a man who is in relation with his natural child or children. When we look at how many children in this world are born fatherless, it breaks my heart, as my children have suffered this epidemic as well. Some men seem to take pleasure in professing that they have children, but they never confess that they are not fathers but "sperm donors" only. I know that term is a bit salty, but it's the truth. Being a father is more than just participating in the conception of a child, but it requires a commitment to another life to which you're responsible. I may date myself with this, but I remember hearing women often say, "momma's baby – daddy's maybe," and didn't get it until it was my own experience.

Have we, as a society, not developed our young men in the area of being a father? Based on conversations with my father before he passed away, he didn't have the best relationship with his father and didn't get the guidance he needed to be a father. Being present only when you want to spend time with the child's mother is not what children need. My dad shared that "grandpa was a rolling stone," and a few DNA tests were needed to answer some questions. My earthly father was mimicking the behavior that he'd seen as a young man, behavior that was deemed normal and acceptable, and it was a lie.

The definition of a father through the lens of a child was harsh. I am grateful for the man that presented unconditional love and guidance in the absence of my earthly father. God does know what we need and provides for us. William was our father by biological standards, but Pop is my father by definition, as we call him. Although he wasn't our natural father, he provided everything for us, from the driving lessons to our first car, to walking me down the aisle on my wedding day.

My brothers, being a father is more than your self-seeking rationalization. It is more than a moment of an oops from pleasing your flesh. Fatherhood is about relationship and accountability, first with God and then with your child. I know many men who have regrets concerning their relationships with their children stemming from many different reasons. Still, the overwhelming hurt is that they allowed the relationship with the child's mother to affect how they treated their child.

A father is bigger than that! Our father said that he succumbed to the pressures of his home life, and that's why he wasn't present in our lives, but we know that's not the truth. He was allowed to be a part-time participant without accountability, and he hasn't been the only one. As women, we also have to take some accountability and value and protect ourselves from the womb seeker.

As I stated earlier, I've encountered my own baby daddy drama. My need for love resulted in giving birth to three beautiful children, two of whom grew up without their natural fathers' participation. This tragedy was at my discretion and due to my pain and ignorance. My sisters, don't harm your children because of your emotional turmoil. Don't deny them a relationship with their fathers because the father doesn't give YOU the time of day. I'm guilty and ask my children for forgiveness often. Not only were they affected, but the fathers were as well.

Our earthly father had been missing in action. Our step-father was the ram in the bush. Our heavenly father continues to be our present help in times of trouble. A father is a necessary component of everyone's life; let's repent of the faulty behavior and be what God requires.

Train up a child in the way he should go,
And when he is old he will not depart from it.
Proverbs 22:6 (NKJV)

REFLECTIONS or THOUGHTS

_____

_____

_____

_____

_____

_____

_____

_____

_____

_____

_____

_____

6 THE END OF THE STORY WAS ANOTHER BEGINNING

When we think about constructing a new home, the first thing is establishing a foundation. Next, you start with the framework and putting up the drywall and insulation. You put down the floors, add fixtures to make it pretty, and then complete the outside or landscape – ensuring that the first impression of your home represents you well. As you complete the job, you will do a final inspection and walkthrough to make sure it fulfills your needs and meets your standards.

As we apply those same concepts to our family – the foundation is our parents and them being in a healthy relationship. If anyone were to do a walkthrough of our build, you might not recognize that it was built with an unstable foundation that has been rebuilt. How were we able to sustain ourselves when we were considered broken from the start? It's the rebuild!

A few months before our father passed, I could sense an urgency in his desire to make the world know us and accept us as his children. He had always invited us to his annual car shows or hunt club dances, but now the participation was more intense. Unlike Valerie, I did not participate in the activities around the passing of my late grandfather, nor did I attend any of the family functions; my foundation was being repaired.

So here we are at the annual Hunt Club season-opening, and we are ALL present. This event was a celebration of our grandfather's legacy, who was one of the founders of the hunt club, which consisted of a collaboration of all of our father's children and grandchildren utilizing the gifts and talents given by God.

I never imagined experiencing a moment

such as this – no contention or strife but rather a time of sharing and embracing our truth. Unfortunately, besides a birthday celebration – the next time we all gathered in the same space was beside our father's hospital bed during his last days on earth.

Here we come to terms with our truth! Here we are, looking into the eyes of our father, filled with emotions. We felt we talked about some of what we felt, but most of the emotions we internalized individually because of the attached pain. We began to recall the good time and the bad times, even the few brief fun moments we share, hoping to overpower the disdain of how we were entreated. The masks are coming off, and every possible misconception is being unfolded.

You are Mine! Those words from my father forever resound in my heart. I've endured days, weeks, months, and years where you, the man who participated in my conception, couldn't or wouldn't receive me as your own but on your dying bed, declares, "You're a good daughter."

The inspectors are showing up, doing a walkthrough of our reality. The questions start again, "When did they become a part of this structure?". The lines of division are apparent, but we remain cordial to keep our father calm. Birthright becomes a focal point, hierarchy in the bloodline, the voice of reason – and we are again silenced.

If I could turn back the hands of time, I would've asked dad to save his breath when he gave us instructions regarding his desires after he passes away. He was experiencing regrets over the handling of his life with each of us. He articulated as best he could, taking short breaths between each interaction, to let us know how he felt, and we, in turn, released any ill will that we may have harbored against him. These interactions should've been a time of reconciliation, but it wasn't. Our father passed away, and we were still left with unresolved emotions and questions. He was the foundation that should've established a loving and lasting relationship for us as his children, yet before my eyes – the house was crumbling.

REFLECTIONS or THOUGHTS

_____

_____

_____

_____

_____

_____

_____

_____

_____

_____

_____

_____

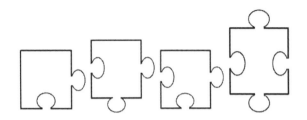

7 PICKING UP THE PIECES

Heal me, O LORD, and I shall be healed; save me, and I shall be saved: for thou art my praise.
Jeremiah 17:14 KJV

To me, the crumbling of the building is reminiscent of a puzzle. As I sit and listen to the words being spoken, I become removed from the situation. Are they aware of what they are saying, or is this their way of trying to put me in "my place"? Who are you to question who I am, or whose I am, to speak out of your mouth, "you don't have proof that you're his"!

Imagine being in the toy aisle at your favorite toy store. You head down the aisle with puzzles all around. Some have big pieces; some are small; some are black and white, and others have a rainbow of colors. Here, you can look at the box to know what you will find on the inside. You know how many pieces are in the box and what age group the puzzle is designed.

With life, our puzzles are not the same. As children, we have no control over how many pieces will be part of our puzzle or how it will look when it's all put together. Will all the pieces fit as they should, or will some be misfits and laid to the side. Our biological father was the border that held all the pieces together. With his death, the pieces began to fall apart.

When the first one falls out, you think it's no big deal, and you go to put it back in place. But now, it no longer fits. Then another falls out, and nothing is the same. How do you fix this, or can it be fixed at all? So often in life, we make choices and say things without regard to how others will receive them. Things change and cannot go back to the way they were. This puzzle needs a new border, but no one is willing to step up to do what is right.

What makes a paper puzzle different from

the life puzzle we live, is our ability to adapt and change. We matured and discover that what we thought was a vital puzzle piece has now changed. Some pieces remain constant, while others are replaced. The newness of life and death causes us to reevaluate our goals and what our puzzle will look like.

Our puzzle was always a forced project. Our father attempted to bring us together every chance he could, but now that he's gone, it's for us to make it happen. It was clear that this was indeed about to end up as two puzzles, not one. The common thread was gone, and the powers on earth were prevailing.

In these last few months, I have learned that shared blood does not always define family, and my family puzzle is beautiful. While we don't all share the same biological connections, those we do share with have created a bond like no other. It's simply an ability to express yourself without condemnation and without questioning who you are.

As we reflect on our life puzzle, we should

solicit Holy Spirit for direction and discernment, as the word teaches us not to put confidence in man. We may have to ask ourselves the question, "Is my puzzle a reflection of me fulfilling God's intent for my life or man?". The words of man destroyed the hopes for completing our puzzle; a merging serene landscape would not be the outcome.

When all else fails, who can we turn to? Who will pick up the pieces? Our heavenly Father is who we should rely on. We may not know why things happen the way they do, but He does. Romans 12:2 reads, *"Do not be conformed to this world, but be transformed by the renewal of your mind, that by testing you may discern what is the will of God, what is good and acceptable and perfect."* (ESV) If we are willing to do his work, our puzzle pieces will again come together, and we will operate in fullness and peace.

REFLECTIONS or THOUGHTS

_____

_____

_____

_____

_____

_____

_____

_____

_____

_____

_____

_____

_____

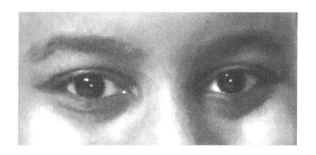

8 FRESH EYES

The light of the body is the eye: if therefore thine eye be single,
thy whole body shall be full of light.
Matthew 6:22 KJV

The morning alarm goes off, and you awake to start a new day. You yawn and wipe the cold from your eyes – and your feet hit the floor. How will this day be different from any other? Will this be a repeat of yesterday, as you allowed stress to overcome you? Will those same doubts of self be relived?

What I have learned and experienced since the death of my parents is that God is truly in control. It is a matter of allowing the Holy Spirit to lead and guide you along your path. As children, we look to our parents for all kinds of support - financial, emotional, and sometimes just a safe place you can go. Now that they are no longer here….my true support system has taken center stage.

Why did it take so long for me to see that? As human beings, we tend to function better if items are tangible. If you can see it and feel it, it is real. Putting our faith and trust in something we can't see or feel is a challenge. You know the trust game; let me fall back and see if you will catch me. Physically, our parents are there to catch us, and it is that same faith that we need to extend to God.

As a spiritual being (praise God), my faith grows stronger each day. I still have family and friends that support me through thick or thin, but MY GOD has never, nor will He, ever leave me. I thank my big sister, Valerie, for being a great example of all that God can do. We were blessed to share the same mother and father. The childhood and adult relationships we shared with each of them may not have been perfect, but they brought to our lives the lessons we needed to learn and the wisdom to understand the importance of breaking curses. A new vision has been placed ahead of me through fresh eyes, and I say, "Holy Spirit, lead the way"! Lead the way on our path of righteousness; lead us on the way of fulfilling purpose; lead the way!

We prayed that some things regarding our family structure might change and that hasn't happened. Are we surprised or bothered? Neither! It is because of the fresh eyes, the eyes of Christ, that we can now understand what being "His daughter" is all about. Beyond the love extended by our earthly parents, the love that covers our sin and the unfailing love of our heavenly Father has empowered us to endure amid all life has to offer, even those things that we enlisted on our own.

If you've had a challenging experience with your earthly father, whether he was present or absent, let us encourage you today with this truth. Psalm 37:23 reads, "The steps of a good man are ordered by the Lord: and he delighted in his way." We don't get to pick or choose our father or mother. We're not fortunate enough to dictate the path we will be placed on or the environment in which we will grow. What we do have the ability to do is have a relationship with God, our heavenly Father. In building that relationship, receiving Jesus as Lord and Savior of your life, your journey towards a healthy future begins.

Fresh eyes gave us the ability to embrace a journey that seemed to be filled with trouble, toil, and turmoil – now realizing the impact of transferred spirits, curses, and belief systems. The implications from lack of a father manifested from generation to generation, making it time for a change. I stated earlier that I had my issues with my children not having a father present in their lives, and I've seen the damage. Still, the greatest failure was me, not allowing them to fuel their relationship with their heavenly Father on their terms.

Parents, please help your children heal from the hurt of a missing father. Don't impose upon your children or the next generations your fear and insecurities. Look at what you've done with fresh eyes and re-align your thinking. With all that we encountered: knowing, yet not acknowledged;

trying to establish relationships as adults; and blending the wrong ingredients for happiness – we were not broken. Today and with every day that follows, we can declare – I AM HIS Daughter!

REFLECTIONS or THOUGHTS

9 EVEN THIS HAD PURPOSE

To everything there is a season, and a time
to every purpose under the heaven:
Ecclesiastes 3:1

On June 20, 2021, my sister Nina transitioned to her eternal rest. Her passing was one of the most challenging moments I've yet to experience in life. Nina, for over a year, walked by faith regarding her health with no complaints. She faced a situation that many would have succumbed to without a fight, but she was a warrior. She was our "Sunshine".

Nina was not only my sister but my confidant, best friend, and my voice of reason. I laughed at myself a few days ago, wanting to call her and share thoughts about the ministry and subsequent moves, realizing that I couldn't. Some suggested that I make the call, but it wouldn't be the same without hearing her respond, "fabulous"!

On the day of Nina's memorial service, I experienced strong emotions, from despair to joy. My siblings were at my side, all but one of them: Zena, Bridgette, Karen, Kevin, and Curtis. This gathering was probably the first time that I could recall having everyone together – and it was all because of Nina.

As you've read our account of life with our father, you saw that Nina's relationship with him and his children was a bit strained, but today, all of that was put aside, and we were family, celebrating her life and legacy.

Nina fulfilled her purpose – serving according to God's plan while alive and in transition, bringing together those who had been estranged. Purpose fulfilled.

There is a time and season to every purpose under heaven, and as believers, we must incline our ears to hear what the spirit of

God is revealing and then be willing to submit to His plan. My sister exemplified that until the end.

If you're in a place of indecision regarding your relationship with your earthly father, heavenly father, or even fulfilling purpose, I want to let you know that I'm here to aid you in a journey of gaining clarity and healing. Before Nina took her eternal rest, she and I had a spiritual visit where she assured me that she was okay, grateful for her life journey, and ready for her reward.

Today, assess your life journey and re-align if needed. Please ensure that you live an intentional life, fulfill your purpose, and take advantage of all that Daddy has for you – You are His Daughter!

.

REFLECTIONS or THOUGHTS

ABOUT THE AUTHORS

Valerie Burrell is an ordained minister of the Gospel and an Apostolic Kingdom leader. She and her husband are founders of Empowerment Place Ministries, where their focus is initiating change in the lives of those who are seeking it through relevant kingdom teaching, coaching, counseling, and mentoring. Valerie is the host of a weekly blog talk radio show, The Empowerment Place, which has a worldwide following. She has completed her MS in Human Behavior and pursuing an MBA. Valerie is the wife of Benny M. Burrell, and they are parents to six adult children and nine grandchildren.

Nina Williams was a former sales professional turned helps professional. She dedicated most of her career to supporting families and providing them with the resources and tools needed to grow, maintain, and sustain their own hierarchy of needs. Born and raised in West Point, Virginia, Nina raised three adult children of her own and stood in the role of youth motivator, advocate, and friend. She was a spiritual force in this world and empowered others to have faith and to trust God. As you embark on this journey with her as a debut novelist, allow her shared experience to inspire, connect, and offer hope for strengthening your anchor. *Written by Ashton Williams*

CONTACT INFORMATION
For booking of the Author, find her contact information below.

Valerie A. Burrell
Email: Empowermentplc@gmail.com
Phone: (304) 306-0522

The Late Nina Y. Williams

I am available for Women's Gatherings, Retreats, Conferences, Empowerment, and Motivational Events.
We also facilitate Marriage and Relationship sessions/coaching.

Made in the USA
Columbia, SC
03 March 2025

54611959R00039